HRH THE PRINCE CHARLES, DUKE OF ROTHESAY

I was enormously touched to have been asked by my beloved Grandmother, Queen Elizabeth The Queen Mother, to be President of The Queen Elizabeth Castle of Mey Trust on its inception as an independent Scottish charity in June 1996.

More than two decades later, the Trust's work is as vital as ever. It has established the Castle of Mey as one of the very few Visit Scotland 5 star visitor attractions north of Inverness. Around 20,000 individuals visit the Castle each year, providing local employment and a benefit to the tourism industry in the region. The far north of Scotland is a magical place and I always enjoy the vast skies and wonderful seascapes which Caithness offers. My Grandmother often remarked that it reminded her of Norfolk, with far-reaching views and a brilliant clarity to the air.

Maintaining an ancient building – particularly one in such a remote and exposed location – is no easy task. It is thanks to the sympathetic way in which the Trustees have managed the upkeep of the Castle of Mey that it retains its special atmosphere. It was, after all, the only home my Grandmother ever owned, and many people comment that her aura still pervades it.

The gardens that Queen Elizabeth so carefully brought back to life in the mid-1950s have blossomed into a remarkable reminder that, however daunting the weather, given a little vision and energy it is possible to maintain a flourishing garden in even the most challenging of locations.

Every year, in late July, I am fortunate to be able to come and stay for up to ten days in the Castle. Quite simply I have fallen in love with it and the local area. I hope that you, too, will enjoy your visit, and that you may take pleasure in the knowledge that, in visiting the Castle and Gardens of Mey, you are helping to maintain Her late Majesty's much loved home for future generations to enjoy. Thank you.

Charles

WELCOME TO THE CASTLE OF MEY

Her Majesty Queen Elizabeth The Queen Mother first saw what was then Barrogill Castle in 1952, while mourning the death of her husband, King George VI. Falling for its ruined isolated charm, and hearing it was to be abandoned, she declared:

"Never! It's part of Scotland's heritage. I'll save it."

Having acquired the most northerly castle on the British mainland, she renovated and restored it, reinstated its original name of The Castle of Mey, and created the beautiful gardens you see today. For almost half a century she spent many happy summers here and shorter visits at other times of the year.

The warmth and affection of the people of Caithness combined with the county's great beauty, meant that The Queen Mother always enjoyed staying at The Castle of Mey. We hope that you too will enjoy the Castle's unique atmosphere.

THE QUEEN ELIZABETH CASTLE OF MEY TRUST
President - HRH The Prince Charles, Duke of Rothesay

Her Majesty
Queen Elizabeth
The Queen Mother

CASTLE OF MEY
CAITHNESS

Elizabeth Angela Marguerite Bowes Lyon was born on 4th August 1900, the youngest daughter and ninth of 10 children of the 14th Earl of Strathmore and his wife, Cecilia Cavendish-Bentinck. She spent a large part of her childhood at Glamis Castle in Angus, the Earl's ancestral home in Scotland. On 26th April 1923, Elizabeth married Prince Albert at Westminster Abbey and became Her Royal Highness the Duchess of York. Their first child, Princess Elizabeth, was born in 1926, followed four years later by Princess Margaret Rose. When Edward VIII abdicated in 1936, Albert succeeded him as King George VI and Elizabeth became Queen. Sadly, her husband's reign was to be tragically short and on 6th February 1952 he died, leaving Elizabeth a widow aged just 51. Now styled Queen Elizabeth The Queen Mother, she retired to Scotland where she fell in love with and restored the ancient Castle of Mey. It was the only home she ever owned in her own right and the summers she spent there continued to give her great pleasure until her death on 30th March 2002, at the age of 101.

*"The rugged glory
of a magnificent coastline."*

Castletown and its harbour was the hub of the Caithness flagstone export industry with the once bustling port providing stone for New York's financial district, The City of London, Edinburgh and Sydney, Australia among many other places. Built in the 1820s by James Bremner with vertical stones to withstand the power of the sea, it now boasts a Heritage Centre and is a haven for birdlife.

St John's Point and nearby Scotland's Haven were favourite picnic spots of The Queen Mother.

The House of the Northern Gate overlooking Dunnet Bay was home to The Queen Mother's friends, Lady Doris and Commander Clare Vyner.

Thurso's East Beach provides the perfect conditions for The Scottish Surfing Championships.

The dunes of Dunnet Bay have created an extraordinary landscape at the head of Dunnet Forest, with its own wildlife and Sculpture Park.

The Island of Stroma lying just off the coast, was once home to fishermen and crofters. The last native islanders left in 1962 and in 1997 the lighthouse keepers left. It is now used for grazing sheep in the summer.

"Caithness is a county of such great beauty, combining as it does the peace and tranquility of an open and uncrowded countryside with the rugged glory of a magnificent coastline.

It is a delight to me now that I have a home here."

Her Majesty Queen Elizabeth The Queen Mother

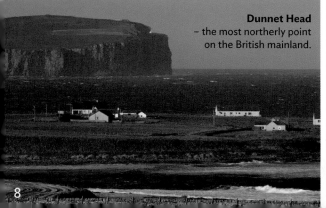

Dunnet Head
– the most northerly point on the British mainland.

A detail of the Castle & its surroundings from the Plan of 1836 to be seen in the Castle's Library.

Castle

William Lithgow
traveller, after being entertained at the
Castle by Sir William Sinclair during
the winter of 1629.

In 1814, the artist William Daniell began his ambitious *Voyage Around Britain*, in Caithness. This aquatint is the earliest known image of the Castle.

HISTORY at a glance

The lands of Caithness were originally held by Jarls or Norse Earls, and from 870 AD onwards they formed part of the Earldom of Orkney and Caithness. The land of Canisbay, on which the Castle stands, is first mentioned in the Letters of Mey in 1508. It is thought to have been built between 1566 and 1572 after George, 4th Earl of Caithness, acquired the Barony of Mey from the Bishop of Caithness.

The Castle's 'Z-plan' design, tower and corbelled turrets are typical of the late 16th century, as are the numerous gun slits throughout the ground and first floors and in the angles of the tower.

In 1572 the 4th Earl granted the lands to his second son, William, who became the 1st Laird of Mey. After only a year he was brutally murdered by his elder brother who was being held prisoner by their father at Girnigoe Castle near Wick. The title and Castle then passed to their brother, George, who founded the Sinclairs of Mey. Ownership of the Castle remained in the hands of the Sinclair family until the 15th Earl of Caithness died without issue in 1889. He bequeathed the Castle and its estates to his great friend P.G. Heathcote and it was later bought from Mr Heathcote's widow by Captain Imbert-Terry.

On the 15th Earl's death the title passed to a relation descended from Sir James Sinclair of Mey, who had been created 1st Baronet in 1631. Malcolm, the present 20th Earl of Caithness, is a direct descendant. In 1996, it gave The Queen Mother great satisfaction to appoint the 20th Earl as one of the Trustees of The Queen Elizabeth Castle of Mey Trust, thereby re-establishing the Sinclair family's link with The Castle of Mey.

James Sinclair, 12th Earl of Caithness was responsible for the addition of the Front Hall, designed by architect William Burn in 1819.

Sinclair was born at the Castle, as was his son Alexander, the 13th Earl and Postmaster General, who was referred to on the Plan of the Estates, to be seen in the Castle Library.

James Sinclair, 14th Earl of Caithness inherited the title in 1855 on the death of his father. He was a Vice-Admiral of Caithness and a Lord-in-Waiting to Queen Victoria. In 1866 he was created Baron Barrogill, taking the Barony's name from the Castle. A great and eminent Caithness character, he was responsible for bringing the first steam-driven car to the county in the 1870s. Less eccentric achievements included the opening of many of Caithness's flagstone quarries, thereby creating employment for the local community.

Left: The Prince & Princess of Wales (later Edward VII and Queen Alexandra) visiting the Castle in 1876 from The Illustrated London News.

1

THE QUEEN MOTHER IN CAITHNESS

2

3

5

12

6

8

9

1. 16th June 1952: The Queen Mother sets foot in Caithness for the first time from a Viking aircraft of The Queen's Flight at Wick Airport, greeted by her friends, Lady Doris and Commander Clare Vyner, of the House of the Northern Gate (3).

2. The early 1950s: 'Barrogill' becomes 'Mey': Having been a WWII billet for troops, the Castle's interior was in a sorry state of repair. There were no bathrooms and just oil lamps and candles for lighting. The Queen Mother set about its renovation.

3. The House of the Northern Gate was where The Queen Mother often stayed before she moved into the Castle.

4. The Royal Yacht Britannia at anchor in Dunnet Bay.

5. The Queen Mother at the Castle with Lady Doris and Commander Clare Vyner.

6. August 1955: The Queen & Royal Family disembark from Britannia in Dunnet Bay to the Castle en route to Balmoral.

7. August 1956: The Queen Mother is presented with the Freedom of Wick as the Seaforth Highlanders form a Guard of Honour. "When I came here I felt at home and among friends."

8. The Mey Sheep Dog Trials plays host to The Queen Mother. Photographed by Wick's John Adams, whose evocative black & white shots helped keep Caithness in the news via *The John O' Groats Journal.*

9. 1960s: The Queen Mother with friends at the annual Mey Games.

13

August 1977: The County of Caithness stages a Ball for The Queen Mother in honour of HM The Queen's Silver Jubilee:

1: Dancing with Major Alan Ferrier.

2. Left to right: Ashe Windham; Lord Glamis (the late 18th Earl of Strathmore); The Queen Mother; Lord Thurso and Sir Ralph Anstruther.

3. In conversation with Sir John Sinclair.

4. 2001: The Queen Mother arrives at Wick Airport.

5. 1990: The Queen Mother in conversation with Sandy MacDonald, Pipe Major of the Thurso Pipe Band, when she received the Freedom of Caithness.

6. At the annual Mey Games: Mrs Bell, the Minister's wife, administers midge repellent.

Designer Norman Hartnell created this ballgown for The Queen Mother. She wore it to the Silver Jubilee Ball in Wick in 1977 (above). The gown remains at the Castle by kind permission of HM The Queen.

1. HM The Queen and The Queen Mother at Scrabster for the last time, just prior to the decommissioning of Royal Yacht Britannia.

2. August 2002: The Castle of Mey opens to the public for the first time.

3. Grandson and Grandmother enjoy a special moment at Scrabster Harbour.

4. 10th August 2002: Prince Charles, Duke of Rothesay, on his first stay at the Castle, unveils the Memorial Bench.

THIS BENCH HAS BEEN PLACED
HERE IN MEMORY OF
**HER MAJESTY
QUEEN ELIZABETH
THE QUEEN MOTHER**
BY HER MAJESTY'S FRIENDS,
TRUSTEES AND EMPLOYEES
AT MEY

QUEEN ELIZABETH LOVED THIS
CASTLE, WHICH SHE SAVED FROM
RUIN IN 1952, SPENDING MANY
HAPPY HOLIDAYS HERE BETWEEN
OCTOBER 1955 AND OCTOBER 2001

Winged faces dating from *c.* 1572 can be seen on the west side of the Tower.

The Queen Mother's cypher decorates the lanterns installed by her in the 1950s.

Edinburgh Sculptor Huw Lorimer created the sandstone panel bearing The Queen Mother's cypher over the south-facing Dining Room window.

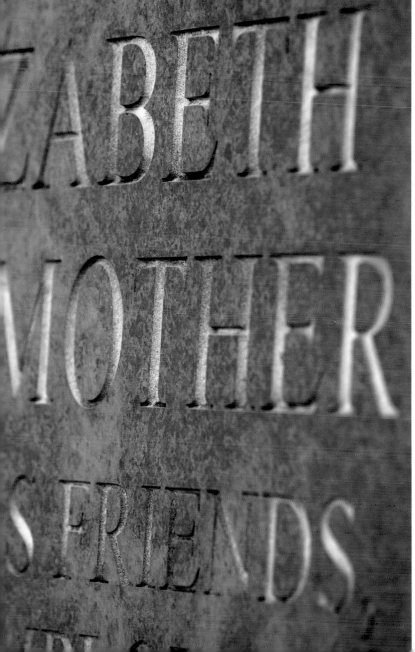

WELCOME TO THE CASTLE

When The Queen Mother bought the Castle in 1952, the interior was very different from the way it is today. She furnished it with items bought locally and others brought up from the south.

She had to have mains water and electricity installed and chose the bathroom fittings herself.

As far as possible, the Castle is still set out very much as The Queen Mother had it.

The guides in the Castle will do all they can to make your visit interesting and enjoyable and are happy to answer any questions you may have.

**Arms of HRH The Duke of Rothesay and (right)
Arms of HM The Queen Mother.**

Her Majesty with David Brown
of the Children's Society, in the Front Hall.

FRONT HALL

Designed by architect William Burn in 1819, the Front Hall was added by the 12th Earl of Caithness. His portrait hangs here with those of other members of the Sinclair family.

Once The Queen Mother's interior renovation works were under way, she consulted a London firm about decoration and curtains. However, the majority of the Castle's furnishings were eventually purchased locally. Much of what you see was acquired in Thurso, either in *Miss Miller Calder's Shop* or in the *Ship's Wheel*. Sadly, these shops are no longer in existence.

The Great Sword of Mey: a 16th century double-handed claymore which belonged to the Sinclair Clan.

The Queen Mother launched *British Queen*
in 1956 and was presented with the bell when the vessel was decommissioned.

The wonderfully extravagant clam shell jardinière – always full of flowers – has been the centrepiece of the Front Hall since The Queen Mother acquired it from Miss Miller Calder's Shop in Wick.

Memories of gardening,
beachcombing and long happy summers
at Mey for The Queen Mother.

The beautiful mosaic of groatie buckies and other shells, featuring The Queen Mother's cypher, was presented by the Gordon family in 1980.

Top: Dunnet Head Lighthouse. Oil on canvas by David Sutherland.

Above: A dabchick (Little grebe) with chicks, one of the stunning watercolour plates in the Front Hall's 'Birds and Flowers of The Castle of Mey and Balmoral' by James Alder in the glass case.

Left: George IV lantern.

DRAWING ROOM

This room was redesigned in 1736 by
Sir James Sinclair, 8th Laird of Mey.
The Queen Mother and her guests
used it every day for afternoon tea,
drinks before dinner or just to read
the newspapers and
listen to music.

A large, late 16th century,
Flemish wool tapestry
hangs on the north wall.

Castle Sinclair Girnigoe.
Oil on canvas by Alistair Sutherland.

A replica stereogram adds period charm with cassettes of The Queen Mother's favourite music.

A playful porcelain bowl holds pebbles and driftwood collected by Her Majesty.

1963: A birthday portrait. The Queen Mother in the Drawing Room, with her corgis, Billy and Bee.

When The Queen Mother was in residence the peat fire in the drawing room was always burning. Much of the furniture came from antique shops nearby, and several paintings by local artists were bought in Thurso and Wick and at exhibitions held by the Society of Caithness Artists. To the left of the George III giltwood mirror above the fireplace are two bold pictures, one by Alexander Sutherland of a seascape near Wick, and the other of Castle Sinclair Girnigoe by his son, Alistair. The carpet was a 90th birthday present from The Queen and is a copy of the original one made for this room. The round inlaid occasional table was made by The Queen Mother's grandson, Viscount Linley, now The Earl of Snowdon.

The original Chinese wallpaper was discovered about 1930 when the room was refurbished. Courtesy of Anne Dunnett, Lord Lieutenant of Caithness.

In addition to the animals in the tapestry, you will notice the tartan 'Nessie', complete with green tam o'shanter, which was placed on top of the tapestry one night by four Irish Guards Equerries after possibly one too many! Although an attempt was made to remove it the following morning, The Queen Mother was so amused that she instructed that it should remain there.

Her Majesty's highly popular and long-serving Private Secretary, Sir Martin Gilliat, would encourage the younger guests to bring back ever more unusual souvenirs from their occasional visits to the Orkneys and elsewhere, as gifts for their hostess. This explains some of the Castle's more eccentric ornaments.

For larger occasions, the double doors between the Drawing Room and the Equerry's Room would be opened to create a space the size of the old hall. On the doors are beautifully ornate ceramic finger plates (left) bearing the cypher of the Earls of Caithness, an original feature retained by The Queen Mother.

The handwritten signatures in the Visitors' Book read:

August 15th 1971

Lilibet
Philip
Charles
Anne

Andrew.

Edward.

STEERING THE LIFEBOAT
OFF SCRABSTER

The Castle of Mey Visitors' Book bears the illuminated dedication: **'FOR QUEEN ELIZABETH THE QUEEN MOTHER, HONOURED AND BELOVED MAJESTY** this Book is made, bound and given as a token of loyalty and gratitude by A. Winifred Scudamore, Malvern – January 1955.'

HM The Queen and her family signed the Visitors' Book having had lunch at the Castle on August 15th 1971. The album photograph shows HM The Queen Mother steering the Scrabster lifeboat.

EQUERRY'S ROOM

When The Queen Mother was in residence, her Gentleman-in-Waiting and Equerry would use this room as an office. Stationery bearing The Queen Mother's Coat of Arms lay on the desk beside Her Majesty's Bible, hymnary and psalter (right). It was the Equerry's responsibility to take these books to Canisbay Church every Sunday.

Stunning views are to be enjoyed from this room across the Pentland Firth to the Orkney Islands.

The writing desk today features photographs of Their Royal Highnesses, The Duke & Duchess of Rothesay.

An excellent portrait of The Queen Mother with her much-loved corgi, Ranger, dominates the Equerry's Room. Painted by the artist Mara McGregor and originally hung in Clarence House, this portrait has been loaned to the Trustees by Her Majesty The Queen. It was commissioned by the Royal Warrant Holders' Association for The Queen Mother's 90th birthday and was presented to her by its President, Barry Reed of the men's clothing retailer Austin Reed, at the former London residence of the Strathmore family in St James's Square. This is the only painting of The Queen Mother with The Castle of Mey in the background.

The Castle with Aberdeen Angus
by Marion Roberts, watercolour 2002.

ABERDEEN ANGUS

HM The Queen Mother with an award-winning Aberdeen Angus cow and North Country Cheviot sheep accompanied by her farm manager the late Mr Donald McCarthy and his two sons, Danny and Sandy.

Renowned throughout the world for its tender and succulent meat, the black Aberdeen Angus has been bred in Scotland for centuries. In 1937, with her husband King George VI, Her Majesty became Joint Patron of the Aberdeen Angus Cattle Society. Over the years she developed her own prize-winning pedigree herd, regularly winning awards at The Royal Highland Show at Edinburgh as well as agricultural shows in the north of Scotland.

The portrait of Castle of Mey Edwina was presented by the Society to mark The Queen Mother's 50 years of Patronage. Ten years later, her 60-year anniversary was celebrated with an Open Day at the Castle and the presentation of the framed collection of photographs to be seen to the right of the desk in the Equerry's Room. The portrait of Castle of Mey Elscot was the Society's present on her 100th birthday.

Also displayed at the Castle are several figurines of celebrated individual cattle. In February 2003 it was announced that The Prince of Wales had taken over Patronage of the Society from his grandmother.

1. Front Hall: This Edward VII ship's chronometer, made by Benzie of Cowes, Isle of Wight, was originally installed on the first Royal Yacht *Britannia*.

2. Front Hall: George III mahogany bracket clock.

THE CASTLE'S CLOCK COLLECTION

The Castle has an impressive collection of clocks of different styles and periods.

3. Front Hall: 'Act of Parliament' clock c.1750, made by Henlett of Bristol. These became known as 'Parliament' clocks, following the imposition of a tax on all timepieces in 1797.

4. Library: Regency rosewood clock.

5. Library: 'Danny's Clock' made by Danny Hughes, the former Housekeeper's son, and given to The Queen Mother on her 100th birthday.

5

8

6. Equerry's Room: George IV mahogany clock.

6

7. Drawing Room: George IV rosewood clock made in Dundee c.1830.

9

8. Drawing Room: Late Victorian clock set within a plinth case surmounted by a tazza.

9. Drawing Room: Second Empire ormolu and bronze mantle clock.

7

10

10. Dining Room: Ormolu mantle clock in Louis XV style.

LIBRARY

In the last few years of her life, The Queen Mother used the Library as her private sitting room and study, decorating it with personal memorabilia, treasured family photographs and gifts.

Books in the room include the old Estate Ledgers from 1891 to 1948 and the Cash Book from 1915 to 1929. The Sinclair Family Bible is here also.

Her Majesty Queen Elizabeth
The Queen Mother when
Duchess of York in 1925.

By Philip de Laszlo
1869-1937

Before The Queen Mother
began renovating the Castle,
this room was the kitchen.
The previous owner, Captain
Imbert-Terry, had decided that
the kitchen should be on this
floor and had moved it from
the ground floor room below.
The Equerry's Room next door
was his dining room.

The Queen Mother's wide
range of interests is reflected
in the choice of books on the
library shelves. Here, books
about Caithness are found
alongside others on subjects
such as gardening, natural
history and horseracing.

During the 1960s and 1970s,
guests were encouraged to
liven up the after-dinner
proceedings by playing the fine
upright walnut piano that The
Queen Mother had bought in
Inverness. Ruth, Lady Fermoy,
one of her Ladies-in-Waiting,
was a classically trained
concert pianist.

1

2

3

4

5

6

7

8

1. George VI: Signed 'Bertie 1943', HM The King is seen wearing the uniform of a Marshall of the Royal Air Force, in the middle period of WWII.

2. The Queen and Princess Margaret: One of three celebrated photographs on top of the piano by Norman Parkinson, one of the Royal Family's favourite photographers. These pictures were given to The Queen Mother by her daughters for her 80th birthday and are signed by The Queen and Princess Margaret.

3. The Queen accompanied by Princes Andrew and Edward.

4. King George VI and Queen Elizabeth with Princess Margaret.

5. The Queen with The Duke of Edinburgh and The Queen Mother in the garden at Mey.

6. Princess Margaret pictured wearing a tiara in an official photograph. In front is a Caithness glass model of The Royal Yacht Britannia.

7. The Royal Family on board MV Hebridean Princess, Stornoway, 29 July 2006, photographed from HMS Argyll by commanding officer, Will Warrender.

8. The Duke of Rothesay at a Highland Games event.

The late 19th century albino hen harrier was probably bought locally.

The Queen Mother spent time here playing after-dinner games such as 'Racing Demon' and, in later years, watching her favourite television programmes such as *Yes Minister*, *Fawlty Towers* and *Dad's Army*. On the wall above the sofa is the 1836 Plan of the Estates of the Earl of Caithness.

QUEEN MOTHER'S
PRIVATE SITTING ROOM

On a tour of the Castle this comfortable and informal room can be seen on the spiral staircase en route from the Library to the first floor rooms.

HM The Queen Mother would use this snug space to write at the bureau or relax.

The window (bottom on the tower pictured right) provides good overhead views of the east garden below.

The coast of Hoy, one of the
Orkney Islands, can be seen
across the Pentland Firth from
many of the bedrooms.

THE BEDROOM FLOOR

Queen Mother's Bedroom
Private Secretary's Bedroom
Queen Mother's Clothes Room
Princess Margaret's Bedroom
Cleaning Cupboard
Guest Bathroom
Lady Doris Vyner's Bedroom
& Commander Vyner's Bedroom

QUEEN MOTHER'S
BEDROOM

Aged 101, The Queen Mother still walked up and down the spiral staircase to her bedroom. This light and airy room has north, south and east-facing windows that enabled Her Majesty to keep an eye, not only on her sheep and cattle, but also on the comings and goings of her guests. The corgis would often sleep on the steps outside her door.

PRIVATE SECRETARY'S
BEDROOM

When The Queen Mother was in residence the Gentleman-in-Waiting would sleep in this bedroom. For many years this was either Sir Martin Gilliat, her Private Secretary, or Sir Ralph Anstruther, her Treasurer.

Lt Colonel Sir Martin Gilliat (1913- 1993) was one of the Royal Household's most efficient and popular members. He was the devoted Private Secretary and Equerry to The Queen Mother for nearly 40 years, having served as Adjutant at Colditz during the last war. He was captured at Calais in 1940.

Major Sir Ralph Anstruther Bt (1921-2002) was Treasurer to The Queen Mother from 1961 to 1998. A Coldstream Guardsman (Second Battalion), he was awarded the Military Cross for operations in Algiers during WWII.

QUEEN MOTHER'S CLOTHES ROOM

Queen Elizabeth and King George VI:
In the passageway are lithographs from paintings by Sir Gerald Kelly RA, begun in 1938 and completed six years later in 1944. Wearing Coronation robes, Their Majesties are depicted in an interior based on the Viceroy's Building, Delhi. The original paintings are in the Windsor Castle Collection.

Although The Queen Mother's clothes were kept in this room, it would sometimes be used as an extra bedroom, especially if the Castle was full of guests. Included in the display are a suit, coat and hat that The Queen Mother often wore when at the Castle.

PRINCESS MARGARET'S BEDROOM

The Queen Mother
hoped that Princess
Margaret would use this
room when staying at
Mey, but although her
daughter rested here one
afternoon, she never spent
a night at the Castle.
The bedroom – which
is said by some to be
haunted – was instead
used by other guests
when visiting Mey.

CLEANING CUPBOARD
& Guest Bathroom

The Cleaning
Cupboard holds
everything needed
to service the rooms
along the corridor.
The items on the
shelves include
boxes of Floris soap,
stoneware hot water
bottles and large
bottles of ink, which
were used to refill
the inkwells in the
bedrooms. Apart
from new carpet
on the floor, the
Guest Bathroom is
fitted out exactly
as it was after being
modernised in 1954.
All the bathrooms in
the Castle, even The
Queen Mother's, are
similar to this.

The Passageway was redecorated in 2013 with wallpaper, fabric and a colour scheme specially chosen by HRH The Duke of Rothesay.

LADY DORIS VYNER'S BEDROOM & Commander Vyner's Bedroom

These bedrooms are named after The Queen Mother's friends, the Vyners, who were among the first guests to stay in the Castle after it had been restored. While Lady Doris slept in the splendid Louis XVI-style bed, its modest size meant her husband would have had to spend the night in the rather smaller bedroom beyond.

Lady Doris and Commander Clare Vyner had the House of the Northern Gate on Dunnet Head. They were the friends who had Her Majesty to stay when she visited Caithness in 1952 after The King died – when she saw the Castle for the first time.

The Castle of Mey from the North-East, a watercolour by Tyall Macinnes.

These west-facing guest bedrooms both have splendid views over the walled garden to Dunnet Head (pictured above).

DINING ROOM

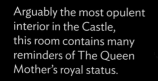

Arguably the most opulent interior in the Castle, this room contains many reminders of The Queen Mother's royal status.

Here, treasured pictures, works of art, gifts and trophies all combine to create a wonderfully elegant yet informal atmosphere.

Artist John Gubbins produced this large decorative watercolour of the Castle and its surroundings for The Queen Mother's 90th birthday. It was presented to her by her friends in Caithness. One of her favourite paintings, it shows the scenes, flowers and animals she most enjoyed whilst here.

The east wall is dominated by the fabulous tapestry of **The Queen Mother's Royal Coat of Arms,** designed by Stephen Gooden RA and woven by R. Cruickshank, R.B. Gordon and J. Louttit at the Dovecote Studios in Edinburgh in 1950.

The Castle from the East Garden by HRH The Duke of Edinburgh, one of a pair of his oil paintings either side of the fireplace.

The Queen Mother was delighted to buy this picture when it was offered to her. Once thought to represent the Royal Yacht of the period, it is now considered to be the S.Y. Francesca, which was acquired by the 15th Earl of Caithness in the Mediterranean in 1883. By I.R. Gray it commemorates the vessel's first visit to the shores of Caithness in 1884. It is unlikely, however, that the yacht would have been moored in shallow water so close to the Castle; so artistic licence was employed. In 1876 (see History at a glance), The Prince and Princess of Wales did visit the Castle and two trees were planted to mark the event. They are still standing.

The beautiful bronze fire-back is by the late Lord Charteris, a talented artist and sculptor, and The Queen's longest serving Private Secretary. He not only designed it, beating out the images in copper on the reverse, but also carried out the casting work himself. This much-treasured piece depicts The Queen Mother's cypher and the Royal Yacht Britannia alongside local flora and fauna such as eider ducks, gannets and terns.

The Sinclair Punch Bowl displayed on the side table next to a Derby dessert service was given to Lord Berriedale, later 15th Earl of Caithness, by tenants and friends of the estate on the occasion of his 21st birthday in 1879. It portrays the Castle, Canisbay Church, Huna Harbour and John O'Groats.

Edward, Prince of Wales, later Edward VII, features in this tapestry firescreen based on a Winterhalter painting.

BUTLER'S PANTRY

To see this remarkable little room is to step back in time to the late 1950s and early 1960s. The period fixtures and fittings evoke memories of Mrs Beaton and Fanny Craddock rather than James Martin and Jamie Oliver!

By adding this room to house all the plates, glassware and cutlery, The Queen Mother found it much easier to entertain guests in the Dining Room next door.

The unusual green baize ceiling was installed as insulation to prevent the noise of cutlery and crockery affecting the Dining Room.

During the working day a footman was always on duty here and it doubled up as the Castle telephone exchange. When dinner was in progress, the plates and food would be kept warm in the old electric oven. The food-lift or dumb waiter, installed to take everything up and down to the kitchen below, was hand-operated. However, the pages and footmen preferred to go up and down the steep stairs rather than listen to the excruciating sounds that emanated from it when it was in use! Because meals could be spoiled by the noise, the lift was rarely used – although there were plans to electrify it and make it silent.

The Butler's Pantry looks west over the walled garden to Dunnet Head, the most northerly point of mainland Britain. Sometimes The Queen Mother and her guests would admire the sunset from this room.

GLASSWEAR

Opposite: Glasswear displaying the cyphers of HM The Queen Mother; HM King George VI; HRH The Prince of Wales. Top Row: Engraved bowl with a Caithness scene; Mey sheep goblet; Castle of Mey engraved glass with The Queen Mother's cypher. Bottom row: Decanters with the cypher of HM King George VI and a Caithness coast engraved bowl.

Each Christmas the children from the local school are presented with a cake from the Castle. The tradition was started by The Queen Mother and is continued today by The Duke of Rothesay.

The classic 'Frigidaire' has been preserved with great care since the late 1950s and still works perfectly today. *The* fridge to have in its day, it was top of the range and very modern for its time.

KITCHEN

Head Chef Michael Sealey greatly enjoyed catering for The Queen Mother in this kitchen.

On good days the sun spills through the south-facing windows, which were nearly always left open when cooking was in progress. In contrast to some other royal kitchens, this one has a splendid view and is exceptionally airy and light.

BREAD

BREAD

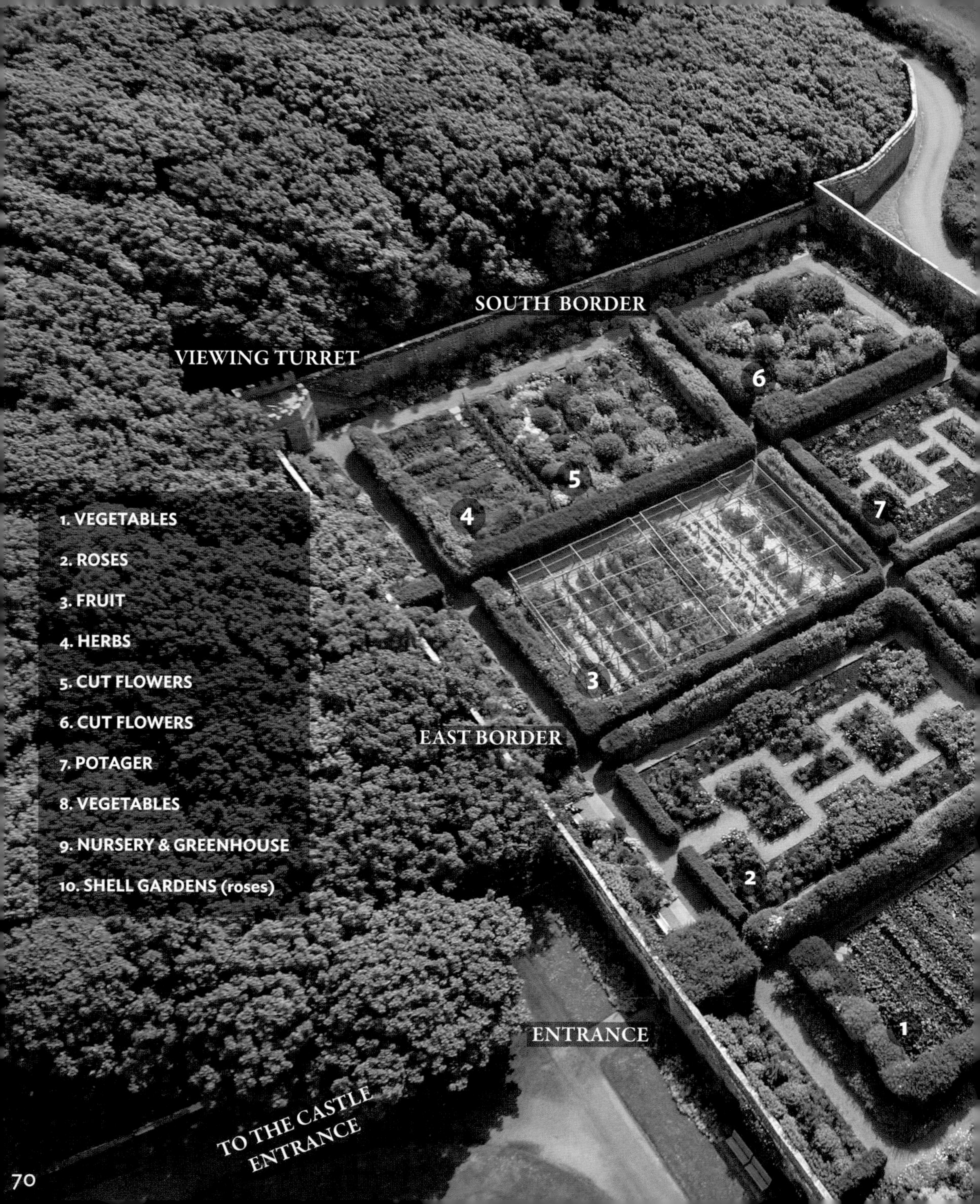

SOUTH BORDER

VIEWING TURRET

6

1. VEGETABLES

2. ROSES

3. FRUIT

4. HERBS

5. CUT FLOWERS

6. CUT FLOWERS

7. POTAGER

8. VEGETABLES

9. NURSERY & GREENHOUSE

10. SHELL GARDENS (roses)

4

5

7

3

EAST BORDER

2

1

ENTRANCE

TO THE CASTLE
ENTRANCE

GARDEN PLAN

Severe winds in this remote part of the country are able to pluck a cabbage from the bleak earth and fling it 60 feet. Without the surrounding 15-foot high 'Great Wall of Mey', this working garden, comprising around two acres, would not enjoy protection from the fierce gales and sea spray that blow in from the Pentland Firth. One advantage of the salty atmosphere, however, is its prevention of too many slugs. The Nursery Greenhouse grows the *Duke of York* variety of peach, a breakfast favourite of HRH The Duke of Rothesay.

Since the Garden was first opened in 2002 there have been several new developments, including the greenhouse on the west wall and a viewing turret in the south-east corner.

WEST BORDER

8

9

GREENHOUSE

10

VISITOR CENTRE

NORTH BORDER

PICNIC AREA

71

The Queen Mother's Garden

The Queen Mother's love of colour in furniture and fashion also found its way into the flowers of the herbaceous borders and the roses in the Shell Garden. Her favourite garden seat is now painted green with a plaque in her memory.

Gardens and gardening were in Her Majesty's blood. Her mother, the 14th Countess of Strathmore and Kinghorne, was a renowned expert. The family homes in which The Queen Mother grew up, Glamis Castle in Scotland and St Paul's Walden Bury in Hertfordshire, both have outstanding gardens.

The Queen Mother's love of gardening started when, as Duchess of York, she took on the garden at Royal Lodge in Windsor Great Park in 1931. After World War II, several other royal houses benefited from her horticultural skills and enthusiasm. As Queen, she planted ornamental trees and shrubs at Buckingham Palace, and created Sandringham's formal garden and large areas of rhododendrons, camellias and magnolias. Despite many difficulties and setbacks, The Queen Mother's experienced green fingers ensured that the garden at The Castle of Mey prospered.

The Flora of Mey

The Queen Mother even managed to nurture her favourite rose, Albertine, into abundance behind an intricate network of four-foot high hedges of privet, currant and elder.

The two sycamore trees were planted by TRH's The Duke and Duchess of Rothesay on 7th August 2005.

The daffodils are abundant in March and April and can be seen lining the South Entrance Drive and the woods.

The garden now consists mainly of hardy perennials and shrubs while old favourites such as primroses, violas and sweetpeas are still abundant. The climbing roses, Albertine, together with nasturtiums and roses, are the highlights of the Shell Garden. One side section on the east side of the garden is made up entirely of old-fashioned shrub roses.

Just on the inside of the Shell Garden door is a deep purple rose – De la Grifferaie – a favourite of The Queen Mother's.

The Greenhouse

A variety of flowers and vegetables are grown in the Greenhouse, ranging from begonias, pelargoniums and lobelia, to succulent ripe tomatoes.

Many of the plants from the Greenhouse and Garden can be purchased in the Visitor Centre Rotunda.

The Castle kitchen benefitted from the wide variety of fruit and vegetables grown here, all chosen for their resistance to wind and sea spray. Raspberries, strawberries, gooseberries, apples, currants, potatoes, peas, beans, carrots, turnips, onions and leeks all thrive here and, for some unknown reason, the exotic globe artichoke does extremely well too! Although The Queen Mother contributed greatly to many royal gardens, it is The Castle of Mey's that is more hers than any other.

Produce Sales

A range of fresh fruit, vegetables and products made from produce from the Garden can be purchased in the Visitor Centre Rotunda.

ANIMAL CENTRE
Just a short walk from the Castle

The original Animal Centre in the Old Granary was established in 2007, thanks to the combination of a generous donation from the Squire family, and the imagination and hard work of the McCarthy brothers, who manage the Castle farm. The wonderful new Animal Centre, situated in the East Woods, was completed in 2016. Great care was taken by the Trust to ensure it was sympathetically built in the local vernacular style so unique to Caithness, using both indigenous materials and local craftsmen.

The poultry section has numerous colourful and eye-catching breeds of bantams and large fowl, including Silver Laced Wyandotte, Lavender Araucana, the ever popular Silkie, Light Sussex, Buff Plymouth Rock, Rosecomb Silver Spangled Hamburgh and The Queen Mother's favourite breed, the massive Buff Orpington. Waterfowl are also represented in the shape of Silver Appleyard, Call ducks and Brecon Buff geese'.

In the paddock there are a variety of unusual sheep breeds in all sizes, shapes and colours: Jacob, Zwartbles, Kerry Hill, Hebridean, Katmoget Shetland, Mule and black North Country Cheviot. The two rare-breed piglets, which are sold locally for breeding at the end of the season, change each year; you might find a Middle White, a Berkshire or a Large Black in residence. The undoubted star of the Animal Centre is Alice the donkey. She can be seen either in the paddock or in her shed when the weather takes a turn for the worse.

Inside are small animals such as rabbits, along with pet lambs; in the first half of the season, helping to bottle-feed the lambs is one of the highlights of schoolchildren's visits. Daisy the wooden cow gives both children and adults an opportunity to try their hand at milking, while an incubator and brooder allow visitors to enjoy hands-on contact with newly hatched chicks and ducklings.

Promoting education and farming is very important to The Queen Elizabeth Castle of Mey Trust and one of its primary aims is to make this varied collection of animals and poultry accessible to as many people as possible. In doing so, this promotes greater awareness and responsible attitudes towards the appreciation of animals and the farming industry. Every year, many local schools enjoy visiting the Animal Centre.

Safety and hygiene are of paramount importance. All the animals are given regular health checks. Hand-washing facilities are available and should be used before leaving the Animal Centre.

VISITOR CENTRE
Tearoom & Shop

On 14th August 2002 The Castle & Gardens of Mey opened to the public, welcoming over 1,200 people on the first day. On day two, 900 people visited, and thereafter the numbers became a little more manageable. Even so, it was soon clear that the creation of a visitor centre with a tearoom and shop was necessary, preferably before the Castle opened again the following season. With that in mind, the Trustees looked at the first design proposal in January 2003... and eventually agreed the final (10th) design in January 2006. We think you'll agree it was worth the wait.

The Visitor Centre was built in memory of Her Majesty Queen Elizabeth The Queen Mother. Designed by Lachie Stewart of ANTA Architecture, Tain, Ross-shire and constructed by DM Geddes, a Caithness firm, it has a Caithness slate roof and floor and is built using Caithness stone with lime mortar and no cement. The result is a building that complements the Castle so perfectly that many visitors assume it has always been there – in fact, it was opened on 4th August 2007 by Their Royal Highnesses the Duke and Duchess of Rothesay.

Opposite below: Their Royal Highnesses The Duke and Duchess of Rothesay unveiling the commemorative plaque in the Visitor Centre, 4th August 2007 watched by Ms Kauffman and her daughter Lauren. *'The construction of this building would not have been possible without the generous support of Ms Julia Kauffman of Kansas City, Missouri and The Gosling Foundation, The Hobson Charity, HIE Caithness and Sutherland and the Annenberg Foundation'.*

The Tearoom serves fresh local produce and enjoys stunning views over to Orkney.

THE CASTLE & GARDENS OF MEY

Inside, enormous Douglas fir beams support the roof, while the walls are lined with larch and 80 cubic metres of sheep's wool provides the insulation.

The under-floor heating is provided by a geothermal system with five bore holes, each sunk to a depth of 100 metres into the ground.

The Shop is unique and sells a wide range of gifts and items, including The Queen Mother's check fabric and also Castle of Mey tweed. All profits from the Tearoom and Shop go to preserving the Castle and The Queen Mother's heritage.

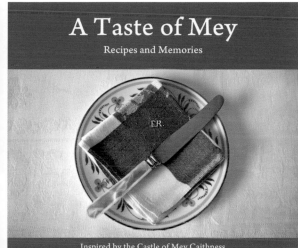

A Taste of Mey

A unique 'Royal ragout' flavoured with marvellous photographs, to be dipped into, treasured and, above all, used. With more than 200 full-colour pages of favourite recipes and personal memories of Her Majesty Queen Elizabeth The Queen Mother from Her friends, members of Her Household, present-day employees of the Castle, and Patrons and Friends of The Castle of Mey.

The Wild Geese – an extract by Nancy McCarthy from *The Taste of Mey*

'*Every October Her Majesty Queen Elizabeth The Queen Mother would return to The Castle of Mey for Her second visit of the year.*

One day whilst going about my duties in the Castle, I met Her Majesty who asked me if I had seen any wild geese arrive for the winter. She then added, "I have seen them every year for fifty years at Mey and I do hope that I see them this year!" I thought for a minute, then replied, "Sorry Ma'am but I haven't seen any yet, but you still have plenty of time to see them before you go."

A few days later I again met Her Majesty, and as She passed me, She whispered, "Still no sign of the geese?" I replied, "No, sorry Ma'am.'

Soon the day arrived for The Queen Mother to leave the Castle. That morning She hesitantly came down the front hall stairs and said Her goodbyes to all the staff. Her Majesty's car drew up outside the front door and just as She was about to step in, to my amazement, a flock of wild geese appeared in the distance. As they flew over the Castle in their V-shaped formation, Her Majesty looked to the sky and Her face lit up. She then turned to us and said, "I'm happy now!"

I knew what She meant. The geese that she had looked for every day had suddenly appeared as if to say goodbye to Her Majesty. Sadly, October 2001 was The Queen Mother's last visit to The Castle of Mey.'

The Legend & Ghost of Lady Fanny Sinclair

Standing in solitary splendour in a field just west of the Castle garden is a stone cross erected in 1840 by Sir Alexander Sinclair, 13th Earl of Caithness, in honour of his great friend and Governor General to India, Charles John Earl Canning. It is, however, better known as 'Lady Fanny's Seat', in memory of the 13th Earl's grand-daughter, Lady Fanny Sinclair.

Fanny loved to go riding every day and was always accompanied by a ploughboy, Andrew Cruickshank. In 1872, at nearly 18 years old, she told her father, the 14th Earl, that she was in love with Andrew and wished to marry him. Andrew was immediately dismissed and exiled to England, and Fanny took to sitting by the stone cross, pining for her one true love. She never got over the loss and one afternoon, five days before her 28th birthday, she threw herself from the top window of the south tower of the Castle. Her crumpled body was carried up to her bedroom, where she died.

It is said that Lady Fanny haunts the Castle to this day: her footsteps have been heard in the passageway on the main guest bedroom floor, where the lights are known to flicker, dim and go out for no apparent reason.

HM The Queen Mother was aware of her ghost and called her "Poor Lady Fanny."

In Loving Remembrance of

Lady Fanny G. E. Sinclair

who died at Barrogill Castle

on 11th October 1883.

Interred in Canisbay Churchyard.

Jesu. Lover of my Soul,
Let me to Thy Bosom fly,
While the gathering waters roll,
While the tempest still is high.

Nothing in my hand I bring,
Simply to Thy Cross I cling.

The Order of Service
for Lady Fanny's
Funeral at
Canisbay Church,
11th October 1883.

Lady Fanny Georgiana
Elizabeth Sinclair
1855-1883.

Jesu, Lover of my Soul,
Let me to Thy Bosom fly,
While the gathering waters roll,
While the tempest still is high.

Nothing in my hand I bring,
Simply to Thy Cross I cling.

CANISBAY CHURCH

After her first attendance in April 1959, The Queen Mother became a regular worshipper at this ancient pre-Reformation kirk – the most northerly place of worship on the Scottish mainland. Like the Earls of Caithness before her, she occupied the Castle Pew in the north transept. The Praise Board was presented by her to the church in 1976.

HM The Queen Mother bids farewell to the Rev.
George Bell, after attending the service in Canisbay
Church for the first time. She was to worship here
for a further 42 years whatever the weather.

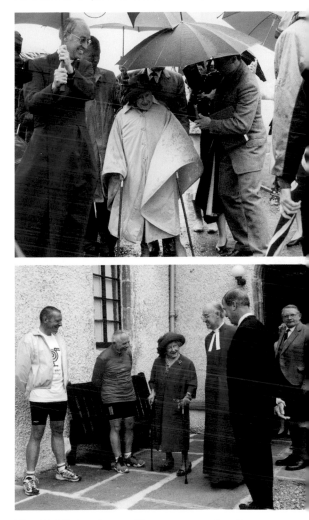

In the mind of the general public John
O'Groats has for many years been most
closely associated with Land's End.
Thousands of long distance walkers and
cyclists have made the 874-mile trek from
Cornwall to Caithness and vice versa in
aid of charity. The name John O'Groats
originated in the 16th century when a
certain Jan de Groot was granted a licence
to operate a ferry between the mainland
and the Orkney Islands for the fee of a
single groat. Jan de Groot died on 13th
April 1568 and was buried here in the
church. His engraved tombstone, originally
situated under the church floor, can be seen
today in the vestibule. Behind iron railings
on the north side of the church is the family
vault of the Sinclairs of Mey. Here a stone
bearing the initial 'S' marks the grave of
Lady Fanny Sinclair, only daughter of the
14th Earl of Caithness. Tragically, both she
and, in 1889, her brother, the 15th Earl,
died young and unmarried, bringing that
line of the Earls of Caithness to an end.

**The highlight of a gruelling sponsored cycle
ride** from Land's End to John O'Groats for a priest
and one of his parishioners, is to meet The Queen
Mother outside the church on a Sunday morning.

PLACED HERE BY
HRH THE PRINCE CHARLES DUKE OF ROTHESAY
IN LOVING MEMORY OF HIS GRANDMOTHER
HM QUEEN ELIZABETH THE QUEEN MOTHER
WHO KEPT SUCH A SPECIAL PLACE IN HER HEART
FOR THIS PARISH AND WHO WORSHIPPED
IN THIS KIRK FOR ALMOST
FIFTY YEARS UNTIL
~ OCTOBER 2001

The Caithness stone memorial to Queen Elizabeth The Queen Mother by sculptor Adam S. Williamson was unveiled on 6th August 2006 by The Duke and Duchess of Rothesay. It now hangs on the wall in the north transept near The Queen Mother's pew.

The Duke and Duchess of Rothesay leave Canisbay Church after attending the Sunday service on 10th August 2008, the day after they were guests of honour at the Mey Highland Games.

The Duke of Rothesay watches a tug-of-war at the Mey Games in 2016.

The Annual Mey Games

As Honorary Chieftain of the Mey Games, The Duke of Rothesay is carrying on the role of his grandmother, The Queen Mother. The Royal British Legion Mey Games are held in August every year in one of the Castle fields, just west of the village of Mey. The event includes traditional events such as piping, Highland dancing, tossing the caber and putting the shot. For many the highlight of the afternoon is the tug-o'-war final, which is usually umpired by the Duke.

BIRDS & wildlife of Mey and the Caithness coast: a snapshot

Wild Whooper swans fly in over Mey from Orkney, October 2016

The huge Gannet is an all-year round resident on the sea at Mey

Fulmars are small Albatrosses – usually seen in summer

Large Grey seals are always close to the beach at Mey

The highly vocal Sandwich tern breeds at sites in Caithness

Oystercatchers inhabit the farmland and meadows

Great northern divers hug the coast and are easily seen at Dunnet Bay

A Common seal pup

Our smallest bird of prey, the Merlin, can be seen at all times, here skipping the waves at Mey beach in 2016

The Ringed plover is a summer visitor to the coast of Caithness

Arctic Long-tailed duck appear in autumn and remain until spring - seen here in Dunnet Bay

Shag & Cormorant are a common sight on the rocky coast

Arctic terns breed nearby

A beautiful spring and autumn visitor – the Greenshank. It also breeds in the flow country near Forsinard

The Puffin – or aptly-named 'Sea Parrot' – breeds at Dunnet Head

Curlew are always present on the coast

Skeins of wild geese are an evocative sight – most usually seen in spring and autumn

Britain's largest bird of prey, the White-tailed or 'Sea' eagle, can be seen at any time around the Caithness coast; if you're fortunate...

The Kestrel is our most abundant and bouyant falcon

The fastest flying bird – the Peregrine falcon – is a regular sight above the skies of Mey

The striking Wheatear favours stony ground

Short-eared owls are a stunning sight on the Caithness moorland

Whimbrel are a delightful migratory bird – a smaller relative of the Curlew

The Common redshank's piping call is the soundtrack of northern coasts

The Lapwing, 'Peewit', or Green plover, is an expert in aerial acrobatics

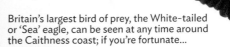

Killer whales (Orcas) are increasingly seen in the Pentland Firth

The rare Iceland gull appears in winter

Book design & photography by Nick Hugh McCann

Written, produced & published by Nick McCann Associates Ltd.
www.nickhughmccann.com/artofheritage
email: hughmcnicholas@yahoo.co.uk

The author and publisher would like to thank the following
for their assistance and contributions:
Clive Richards, author of *The Queen Mother and Family at Home in Caithness*;
Barbara Hiddlestone, Trust Historian & Archivist, for her research
material and text on the Castle's history and architecture;
Dr Iain Macnee, former Minister of Canisbay Church;
Jane Pruden, editorial.

Additional pictures by: John Adams, courtesy of North of Scotland Newspapers; Bridgeman Art Library; Getty Images;
Shirley Farquhar; Tony Gorzkowski; J. McDonald Photographers, Wick; Rex Features; RSPB Images; Peter Smith.

The objectives of The Queen Elizabeth Castle of Mey Trust include the preservation of historic buildings,
the advancement of historical and architectural education, the development of the Aberdeen Angus breed of
cattle and North Country Cheviot breed of sheep, and other projects for the benefit of the community.
President: HRH The Prince Charles, Duke of Rothesay.

ISBN-13: 978-0-9516891-7-2